BUSH FLYING

BUSH FLYING

DAVID OLIVER

Published in 1988 by Osprey Publishing Limited
27A Floral Street, London WC2E 9DP
Member company of the George Philip Group

British Library Cataloguing in Publication Data

Oliver, David
    Bush flying.—(Osprey colour series)
    1. Canada. Remote rural regions. Air services.
    Float seaplanes.
    I. Title
    387. 7′3347′0971

ISBN 0-85045-867-6

Editor Dennis Baldry
Designed by Paul Butters
Printed in Hong Kong

Front cover lucky passengers enjoyed two
wonderful experiences at the same time: a trip
through Alaska's beautiful glacier world and a
ride in the classic Beaver floatplane. Ketchum
Air Service returns them safely to Anchorage.
(Courtesy Karl Heinz Morawietz)

Back cover Nautical but nice: Harbour Air
Cessna 185 taxies past a variety of local vessels
at Vancouver Harbour

Title pages A Cessna O-1 Bird Dog gamely
struggles to unstick from the still waters of Seal
Cove

A Maule Skyrocket, an unlikely air ambulance
belonging to the Canadian Wings of Hope
organization, seen at Belize International in 1986
waiting for a new propeller. Formed in 1972, the
non-profit making Wings of Hope fly mercy
missions to remote parts of South and Central
America. Its six aircraft are flown by volunteer
US and Canadian pilots

Ethiopian Airways' DHC Buffalo landing at Addis Ababa in January 1988. On this occasion it was carrying Ethiopia's President Mengistu for whom a single green velvet seat had been installed forward of the more usual canvas variety

Contents

Otter and Twin Otter

The seaplane base at Campbell River on Vancouver Island, British Columbia. Campbell River is the centre for the logging industry in the area and a popular resort for salmon fishing. 'Salmon Lodge', a favourite haunt of John Wayne and other sport fishing personalities, was situated close to the seaplane base

Top left Large numbers of rugged DHC-3 Otter (foreground) and DHC-2 Beaver floatplanes support the logging and fishing industries in British Columbia

Left Two 8-10 seat Otters belonging to CoVal Air, the largest floatplane operator out of Campbell River. C-FAPQ is an ex-Wideroe of Norway machine while C-FQEI in the background is an ex-US Army U-1A

Above One of CoVal Air's three Otters used on scheduled flights, known as skeds, and available for charter at CAN$375 per hour

11

Top left Trans Provincial Airlines operate four amphibious Otters out of Prince Rupert in northern BC. One is seen here undergoing maintenance at the company's base at Seal Cove, Prince Rupert, in November 1987

Left CoVal Air Otter C-FAPQ, powered by a 600 hp Pratt & Whitney R-1340 radial engine, docked at the airline's Campbell River base

This page An Air BC DHC-6 Twin Otter floatplane at the airline's Vancouver Harbour Terminal in October 1987

Overleaf, left inset Vancouver Harbour seaplane base with an Air BC Twin Otter 200 in the foreground. Air BC uses four twenty-year-old Twin Otter floatplanes on scheduled services to Victoria Harbour on Vancouver Island. The Duke of Edinburgh flew in this aircraft a few days after it was photographed while attending the Commonwealth Conference in November 1987

Overleaf, right inset Two of Air BC's Twin Otter 100 floatplanes at Victoria Harbour located on the southern tip of Vancouver Island

Overleaf, main picture Vancouver Harbour seaplane docks with Air BC Twin Otter 100 (foreground) and a Harbour Air Cessna 185

These pages Air BC Twin Otter landing at Burrard Inlet at the end of the 30 minute flight between Victoria and Vancouver Harbours

Top left A Twin Otter floatplane undergoing maintenance at Harbour Air's base on the North Arm of the Fraser River which runs alongside Vancouver International Airport's South Terminal

Left Untieing one of Harbour Air's two Twin Otters as the PT6A turboprops are wound-up

This page A Harbour Air Twin Otter moored at the airline's Fraser River terminal

Overleaf A Rwanda-registered Red Cross Twin Otter 300 awaits the arrival of a famine relief team at Addis Ababa in January 1988

Above Three of Ethiopian Airlines' six Twin Otter 300s on the ramp at Addis Ababa's Bole International Airport. The airline provides the only link between the capital and many outlying towns in remote parts of the country

Top right Adorned in the distinctive colour scheme of Ethiopian Airlines, this Twin Otter arrives at Addis after a scheduled flight to Jimma

Main picture An Ethiopian Airlines' Twin Otter taking off from Gondar's dusty airstrip, situated high in Ethiopia's Central Highlands. The strip has a mind-concentrating sheer drop at the far end

Beaver

Seen taxying into Seal Cove at Prince Rupert, British Columbia, to refuel is a US registered Beaver from Alaska

N1433Z drifting into the Seal Cove seaplane base. The smart US Beaver from Enchanted Lake, Alaska, has a weight-saving Hartzell 3-blade prop, polished spinner and square rear window, all fitted by the west coast seaplane specialists Kenmore Air Harbour Inc located near Seattle, Washington

Overleaf, main picture Another Kenmore modified US Beaver, operated by Iliamna Air Taxi Inc of Alaska, refuels at Seal Cove in October 1987 during a flight from Alaska to Seattle to beat the winter weather

Overleaf, inset Iliamna Air Taxi flies schedules and charters from Iliamna Lake located at the top of the Alaska Peninsula some 150 miles southwest of Anchorage

Left A North Coast Air Services' Beaver slides out of Seal Cove as the morning mist hugs the surrounding hills. The airline's boss, Jack Anderson, is one of the old breed of bush pilots. With a reputation for having a short fuse, Anderson, who flew Lancasters over Germany during World War 2, lost a son in a floatplane accident a few years ago

Below The North Coast Beaver taxies out of Seal Cove at the start of a scheduled flight from Prince Rupert to Port Simpson

A family of American Indians climb aboard a
North Coast Beaver docked in front of the
airline's log-cabin terminals at Seal Cove,
Prince Rupert. The airline operates daily
schedules and charters throughout the Pacific
Northwest all year round

The 450 hp Pratt & Whitney R-985 Wasp bursts into life as North Coast's Beaver C-FEYN prepares to leave Seal Cove for the Indian village of Kitkatla

Overleaf, main picture One of North Coast Air Service's three Beavers taxies across the mist shrouded flat calm waters of Seal Cove

Overleaf, insets The North Coast Beaver drifts into Seal Cove past the old wooden jetty

Trans Provincial Airlines, part of the Jim Pattison Group which owns Air BC, is the biggest seaplane operator based at Seal Cove. C-FTCW, one of the airline's six Beavers flying out of the Prince Rupert base, waits for its first passengers of the day

Overleaf, main picture A Trans Provincial Beaver prepares to leave Seal Cove seaplane base as a North Coast Beaver arrives

Overleaf, inset A Trans Provincial Beaver lands in Seal Cove against a background of log-rafts and high rise hills

Trans Provincial Flight CD602 arrives at Seal
Cove from Bella Bella, 185 miles to the south,
into the low autumn sun

Above Two smart seaplanes at Seal Cove, a Trans Provincial Beaver in the foreground and a fisheries Cessna 185

Top right An overall view of Seal Cove seaplane base at Prince Rupert, BC

Right Refuelling a North Coast Services Cessna 180 as the early morning mist hangs over Seal Cove

Overleaf North Coast (foreground) and Trans Provincial Beavers arrive at Seal Cove within seconds of each other. All scheduled flights from the busy seaplane base, which has no ATC, are conducted under VFR whatever the weather. The three main operators at the seaplane base, all of which use different radio frequencies, fly some fifty skeds a day

An early production Beaver belonging to Burrard Air, which operates between Vancouver International's seaplane base on the Fraser River, to Nanaimo and Salmon Arm on Vancouver Island

The pilot of G W Cox & Sons Logging Ltd's Campbell River based Beaver pumps water out of the floats before the first flight of the day

These pages Cox's smart Beaver leaving its
Campbell River base taking a logging crew for a
10-day stint at a remote logging camp on the
mainland. C-GFDI, ex-USAF U-6A, had recently
returned from Kenmore Seaplanes Inc where it
was given a reconditioned balanced engine, 3-
blade Hartzell prop, polished spinner, enlarged
rear window and smart new paint job

Top left Another airline supporting the logging industry out of Campbell River with Beaver floatplanes is Vancouver Island Air

Left and above Another Jim Pattison floatplane company, Pacific Coastal, operates amphibious Beavers on skeds between Vancouver Island, Port Hardy, Ocean Falls and Campbell River. C-FGQW, an ex-US Army U-6A Beaver, picks up a logging crew and its equipment from Campbell River

A very executive Beaver belonging to a local logging company sports a large spinner, twin-rear windows, streamlined floats and tail strake (compare with Beaver on preceding pages), and immaculate colour scheme, taxies past the Campbell River seaplane traffic sign

Left One of Powell Air's two Beaver floatplanes at the company's Vancouver Harbour base. Note that the prop blades are positioned at the horizontal to prevent water settling in the tips

Below The Powell Air skeds, Vancouver – Victoria – Powell River, painted on the Beaver's door beneath the pilot's bubble window

Overleaf Powell Air's base is located on Harbour Road within sight of Vancouver's high rise skyline

KEEP
TAP
SHUT
OFF

Above Beaver and Cessna 185 floatplanes at Harbour Air's maintenance base located on the south side of Vancouver's International Airport

Top right Two of Harbour Air's five Beaver floatplanes at the Fraser River seaplane base situated alongside Vancouver International Airport

Right An early production Harbour Air Beaver fitted with deep, and battered, strake under the rear fuselage instead of the more popular finlets

Overleaf Another Harbour Air Beaver docked at the Fraser River base. The Beavers fly summer skeds from Vancouver to six of the Gulf Islands off the southeast coast of Vancouver Island

CoVal Air operates to a total of 160 points along British Columbia's Pacific Coast—more than any other airline in Canada! Its fleet of Otter, Beaver and Cessna floatplanes fly as far south as Vancouver and as far north as Rivers Inlet serving the logging community the year round, and fishing and tourism during the summer months

Overleaf A privately owned Beaver floatplane parked on Toronto Island Airport's seaplane ramp. Overshadowed by the city's skyscrapers, the Beaver is used by its owner for fishing trips to Ontario's numerous freshwater lakes

Above Developed in 1960, the Turbo Beaver III, powered by a 578 shp United Aircraft of Canada PT6A turboprop, sold in small numbers to bush operators in North America. Tyee Airways of Campbell River operate one of the sixty Turbo Beavers sold on services to Vancouver, Nanaimo and Jervis inlet

Main picture Tyee's Turbo Beaver gets on the step during take-off from Vancouver's Burrard Inlet

Cessna

One of Powell Air's smart Cessna 180J Skywagons taxying into Burrard Inlet to take-off for a local sightseeing flight

Overleaf Powell Air's two Cessna 180 floatplanes fly local skeds, charters and scenic tours from Vancouver Harbour

Manhandling a Harbour Air Cessna 185F Skywagon II at the airline's Vancouver International seaplane dock. Harbour Air, one of the largest floatplane operators in British Columbia, fly a dozen scheduled routes in the area

Left A Harbour Air Cessna 185 touches down at the crowded Burrard Inlet seadrome with a police escort

Above A Cessna Skywagon II at Harbour Air's main base at Vancouver International's seaplane dock on the North Arm of the Fraser River

The pilot gives a Harbour Air Cessna 185 a
thorough pre-flight inspection at Vancouver
Harbour

Harbour Air Cessna Skywagon C-GUKZ taxies
out of Vancouver Harbour at the end of a busy
day to return to the compay's base on the south
side of Vancouver International

Above An evening return to its Sausalito base in San Francisco Bay for one of Commodore Seaplanes Cessna 180s

Top right Commodore Seaplanes mixed fleet of Cessna 180s and 206s (foreground) fly coastal tours and fishing charters in the San Francisco area from Sausalito, California

Right Sunset Coast Marine Ltd's Cessna U206 Stationair docked at Vancouver International's seaplane base on the North Arm of the Fraser River

Top left North Coast Air Services flies a weekly supply flight from Prince Rupert to the caretakers, two English couples, of a deserted mining town at Kitsault, close to the US-Alaskan border. Overshadowed by the 9000 ft snow topped peak of Mt Pattullo, the 30-year-old Cessna is unloaded by its 23-year-old pilot—for much of the year the isolated caretaker's only link with the outside world

Left One of only four on floats, an ex-US Army Cessna O-1 Bird Dog tied up at the Seal Cove seaplane dock at Prince Rupert while en route from Alaska to Seattle. Note the original Army olive-drab showing through the worn paintwork on the nose

Above The rare US-registered Bird Dog seaplane taxies out into Seal Cove at the start of a long haul to the United States. The extra drag created by the Bird Dog's Edo floats reduce its cruising speed to little more than 80 knots

Harbour Air is the largest Cessna Skywagon floatplane operator in British Columbia with a fleet of eleven. Two of the Cessnas are seen here at the airline's maintenance base at Vancouver International Airport

Left page A brand new US-registered Cessna Caravan 1 operated by Air-Serv International at Ethiopia's Addis Ababa Airport supporting famine relief agencies in January 1988

This page The 14-seat Caravan 1, powered by a 600 shp Pratt & Whitney (Canada) PT6A turboprop, was designed as a replacement for the ubiquitous DHC Beaver/Otter family. The aircraft illustrated is the second of Air-Serv International's Caravan 1s based at Addis Ababa in January 1988

Goose and Mallard

Trans Provincial Airlines continue to operate a fleet of three Grumman Goose amphibians on scheduled passenger services out of its Seal Cove base at Prince Rupert, British Columbia

Overleaf Trans Provincial's Flight CD310 from Sandspit in the Queen Charlotte Islands touches down on the back-waters of Seal Cove and waddles up the seaplane ramp at the airline's Prince Rupert Terminal

Grumman Goose C-FEYN, seen in its striking Trans Provincial Airlines livery at Seal Cove in October 1987, was built in 1942 and delivered as a Goose 1A to the Royal Navy as FP507. It later served with Air West and Air BC and was fitted with retractable floats

N324, an ex-US Army JRF-5 Goose built in 1944, seen here with fixed floats at the San Pedro seaplane terminal in colours of Air Catalina in 1978. The airline ran scheduled passenger services with six Grumman Goose amphibians to Catalina Island, off the coast of southern California, from San Pedro until the early 1980s

Top left Another ex-US Navy JRF-5, N1257A belongs to Catalina Seaplanes, flying regular cargo flights and charters between Long Beach Airport, California, to Avalon Bay, Catalina Island. The Goose is seen at Long Beach before a major paint job in November 1986

This page Catalina Seaplanes second Goose, N69263, after its re-paint at Long Beach. An ex-RN Goose 1A, FP482 was built in 1942

Left An anonymous long-nosed Goose with fixed floats named *Loose Goose*, at Long Beach in November 1986

Overleaf This immaculate Grumman Goose is the longest serving aircraft with the Royal Canadian Mounted Police Air Section. The Mounties took delivery of the ex-RCAF amphibian in April 1946 and have operated it ever since. From 1975 C-FMPG has been based at Seal Cove, Prince Rupert and is currently flown by Special Constable Don Sundin. Used to transport police specialists to remote parts of the Pacific Northwest, the Goose is flown all year round despite being restricted to VFR-only flights. Although equipped with Loran C, it has no HF radio or autopilot, though long flights of up to five hours duration are not uncommon

North Coast Air Services derelict Grumman Mallard C-GHDD *Patricia*, reputed to have been used as a flying whore-house by isolated logging camps in north western BC during the 1960s. Pictured at Seal Cove in October 1987, the Mallard was purchased by the Vancouver-based airline Wagair, which intends to put it back into service

Dakota

Inset An Ethiopian crow perches on the beautifully painted tail of an Ethiopian Airlines' DC-3 at Addis Ababa

Main picture Two of Ethiopian Airlines' domestic fleet, a DHC Twin Otter and a DC-3, on the ramp at Addis Ababa Airport—which is 7625 ft AMSL

Above One of Ethiopian Airlines' fleet of eight Dakotas, ET-AIB, starts up at Addis Ababa in January 1988. Built in 1946, this ex-Comm Airways DC-3D flies a scheduled passenger service to Dire Dawa, 220 miles to the east of the capital

Right page ET-AGT, a C-47A delivered to the RAF as KG744 in 1944, seen at Ethiopia's newest airport of Bahar Dar on a charter passenger flight from Addis Ababa in January 1988. Bahar Dar, located 385 miles north of Addis on the southern tip of Lake Tana, is being developed as a possible tourist centre

Above Ethiopian Airlines' Dakota freighter ET-AHG parked at Gondar airstrip. Another ex-RAF C-47A (KG794), 'AHG was bought from AD Aviation Ltd in 1979 and currently flies cargo between Gondar and Humera in Eritrea

Below ET-AHG in front of the terminal building at Gondar where the airstrip runs into the main street of the village in the background

Overleaf, main picture Ethiopian Airlines Dakota ET-AGT parked at Gondar overlooking the Central Highlands. Situated 450 miles north of Addis Ababa and almost 8000 ft above sea level, the walled city of Gondar was Ethiopia's ancient capital

Overleaf, inset The view from Ethiopian Airlines' Dakota ET-AGT as it flies over the country's Central Highlands, which can rise to 14,000 ft. The unpressurised DC-3 cruised at 11,000 ft during the 1 hr 30 min flight between Addis Ababa and Bahar Dar

Left Seen on the dump at Addis Ababa Airport in January 1988 is Dakota ET-AHS—an aircraft with an interesting past. Built in June 1945 it served with the USAF, the Portugese Air Force, starred in the motion picture *A Bridge Too Far*, and was acquired by Sweden's Count von Rosen to fly food to famine areas in 1974 as *The Helping Lion*. After the Count's death in 1977 at the hands of Somali troops at Gode, it was operated by the Ethiopian Government's Relief and Rehabilitation Commission (RRC)

Top left ET-AGT on the apron at Addis Ababa in January 1988. The 44-year-old C-47A is normally used for carrying freight to Goba but can be fitted with canvas bench seats for 26 passengers

Above Undergoing a 200-hour check at the company's main base at Addis Ababa in January 1988 is Ethiopian Airlines' oldest Dakota—ET-AHQ. Built as a C-47 for the USAAF in August 1942, it served with the Yemen Arab Republic Air Force prior to joining Ethiopian Airlines in 1981

One of two ex-Ethiopian Air Force Dakotas recently transferred to the RRC based at Addis Ababa. ET-AJG (formally '701'), had been operated by the Air Force since 1947. The RRC supports the Government's famine relief programme and resettles refugees from drought stricken parts of the country in more fertile areas

One of the older Dakotas still flying scheduled passenger services in Canada is Perimeter Airlines' C-FFAY. Built in 1942, she operates from Winnipeg to points in Manitoba and Saskatchewan and is seen here lining up beside a Convair 440 undergoing a major rebuild

C-FFAY is joined at the Winnipeg holding point by one of Northland Air Manitoba's four DC-3s. C-FIKD was delivered to the RAF as KP266 in 1945 and following a recent rebuild was fitted with panoramic rear windows. The Dakotas fly to a number of Indian Reservations with such names as *Red Sucker Lake*, *Garden Hill*, *God's River* and *God's Lake Narrows*

Commando

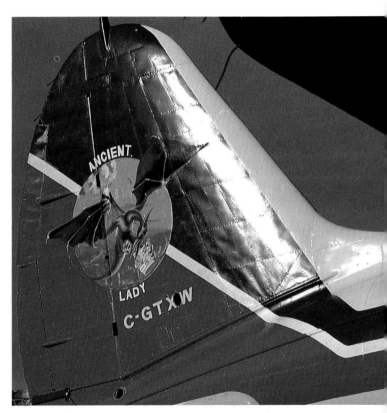

Above Air Manitoba operates one of the largest fleets of C-46 freighters in North America and C-GTXW *Ancient Lady*, delivered in October 1987, is the latest addition to the airline's fleet of four Commandos

Left and overleaf Air Manitoba's *Ancient Lady* nearing the end of an extensive rebuild at Winnipeg before joining the airline's cargo fleet

Left and overleaf Northland Air Manitoba, formally Ilford-Riverton Airways, operates cargo services in northern Manitoba and the Arctic with Curtiss C-46 Commandos. Powered by two 2000 hp Pratt & Whitney R-2800 radials, the 45-year-old C-46 can carry a useful 16,000-lb load of freight

Left page The bulbous shape of C-GIXZ stands on the Air Manitoba ramp with its cargo doors open. Note the tracked loading trolly parked under the wing

This page CF-FNC, a well-weathered Air Manitoba C-46F Commando freighter follows a Perimeter DC-3 out to Winnipeg's main runway in November 1987. The veteran Commandos often work out of 3500–4000 ft clay strips in northern Manitoba

Overleaf The early morning sunshine shows up the polished metal finish of C-GIXZ. The C-46 is parked in front of Air Manitoba's freight sheds at Winnipeg Airport. More than 200 of the 3160 Commandos built during World War 2 remain active in North and South America

Last page The tail of Northland Air Manitoba's C-46 freighter reveals C-GIXZ's former US identity—N7923C